Super Sculptures

Written by Tash

Illustrated by Antony Elworthy

Contents

Collins

What is a sculpture?

A sculpture is a work of art.
It's something made by a person.

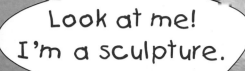

3

What shape is a sculpture?

A sculpture can be any shape.
This one has a spiral shape.

It spirals out into the sea.

4

Spiral Jetty by Robert Smithson, 1970

What size is a sculpture?

A sculpture can be any size.
This one is 93 metres tall.

This famous sculpture is in New York.

The Statue of Liberty by Auguste Bartholdi, 1884

What is a sculpture made from?

A sculpture can be made from any material.

This one is made from fur.

Object by Meret Oppenheim, 1936

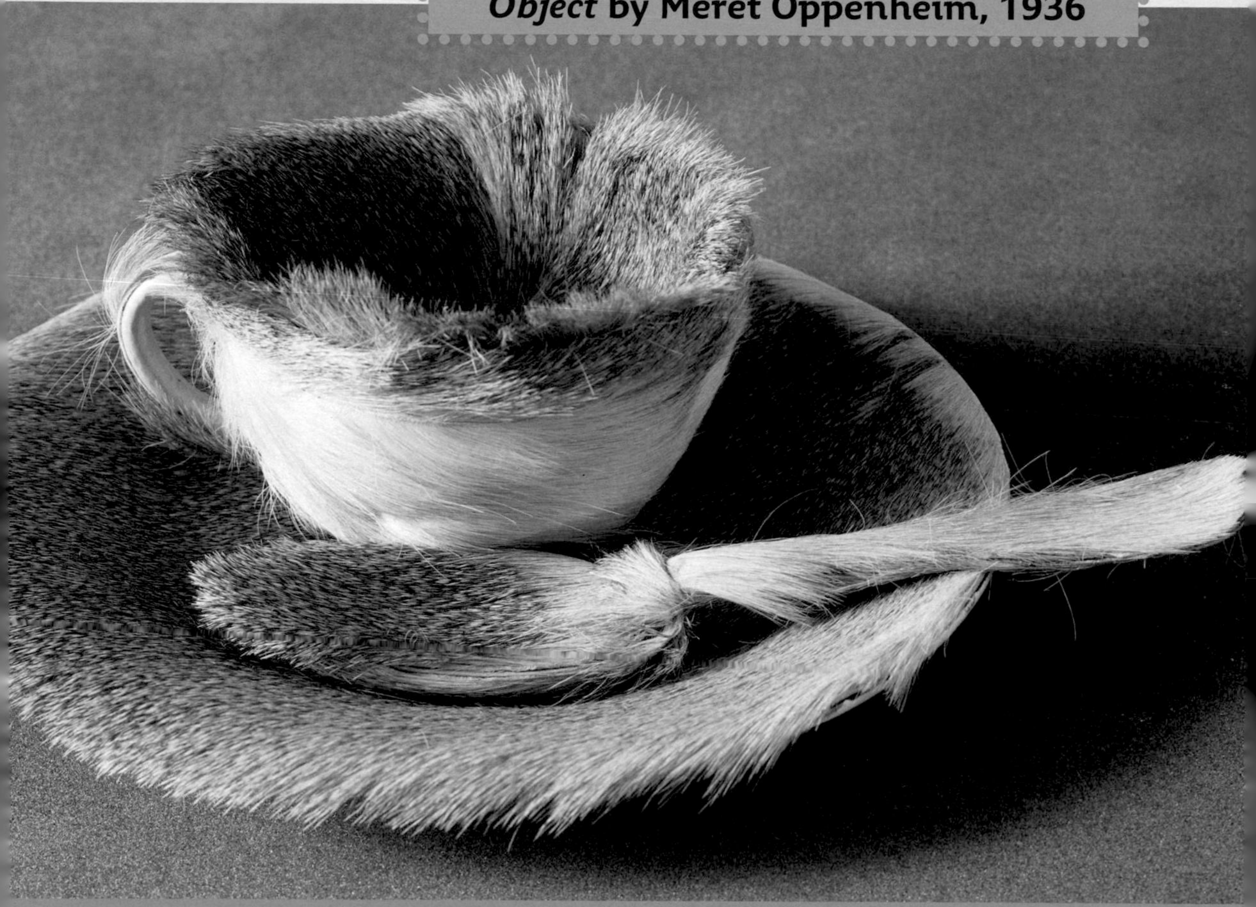

This sculpture is made from the electrical junk that people throw away.

What can I make from this lot?

WEEE Man by the RSA, 2005

How is a sculpture made?

A sculpture can be made in lots of different ways.
This sculpture was made by filling a real house with concrete and then taking the roof and walls away.

House by Rachel Whiteread, 1993

This sculpture was made from bronze.

King and Queen by Henry Moore, 1952–53

Some sculptures help you to look at things in a new way. This sculpture was made by wrapping a bridge up in cloth.

The bridge looks like a present.

How long do sculptures last?

Some sculptures last for a long time. This one is in Egypt.

It's thousands of years old.

The Great Sphinx, artist unknown, about 2540 BC

Some sculptures last for a short time.
This hotel is made from ice.
Every spring, it melts, and every
winter, a new hotel is made.

Brrrr!

The Ice Hotel in Sweden

Goodnight!

Sculptures can ...

... be any shape.

... be very tall.

... be made from fur.

... be made from junk.

... be made in
different ways.

... be made from bronze.

... help you to look at
things in a new way.

... be very old.

... melt.

:paw: Ideas for guided reading :paw:

Learning objectives: use a range of cues to work out, predict and check the meanings of new words; predict what a book may be about from the cover; note the features of non-fiction texts; blend phonemes in words with clusters for reading; read and discriminate words with the initial cluster 'sc'; take turns to speak, listening to others' suggestions and talking about what they are going to do.

Curriculum links: Art – sculpture; Design & Technology – developing and planning ideas.

High frequency words: be, made, from, out, about, some, what, one, house, then, help, by, last, new.

Interest words: sculpture, jetty, spiral, helicopter, famous, material, object, electrical junk, concrete, bridge, thousands, sphinx, melts.

Word count: 272

Resources: small whiteboard and pens, modelling clay.

Getting started

- Look at the cover of the book and ask the children what the photo shows. Collect their words used to describe the sculpture.

- Read the title with the children. Ask them for ideas about sculptures, and any examples of sculptures that they know.

- Explain that this is a non-fiction book that will give information about sculptures. Ask them what sort of information they would expect to find.

- Ask the children what features they would expect to see inside a non-fiction book (*contents, headings, labels, photographs*).

Reading and responding

- Walk through the book together, looking for typical features of non-fiction books.

- Read the questions on the contents page together and ask the children to choose a question to find the answer to.

- Model how to use the contents to turn to the correct page, using page numbers and skimming/scanning techniques.